DuckDB Data Ingestion

Importing Delimited Text, JSON, and Parquet files

Djoni Darmawikarta

Table of Contents

Introduction

Welcome to **DuckDB database: Data Ingestion**

DuckDB is an open-source relational database. It is an embedded database. There's no database server; all you need to create and access all database objects is a client.

Currently, clients are available for R, Python, Java, Julia, C, C++, Node.js, ODBC, Wasm, and CLI (Command Line Interface).

We will use the CLI client in this book.

When you run **duckdb bookdb** in the CLI as shown on the screenshot below, a **database** named bookdb will be created.

And, as soon as you create a database object, such as a schema, a **file** named bookdb will be created. The screenshot below showing the bookdb database is what I see in my computer.

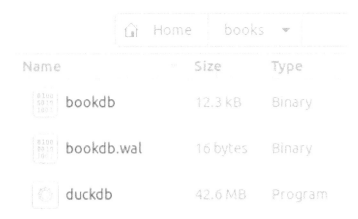

The bookdb file contains all the objects required by the database to function. Another file, bookdb.wal, is a temporary file created for rolling back transactions; it will automatically be deleted when you exit the CLI. (the file type wal stands for write-ahead-log)

Once the database objects are created, multiple clients can read-only access the database at the same time. At one time, a client can maintain (update), the database.

DuckDB is designed to support OLAP (Online Analytic Processing) workload. In OLAP data is generally loaded in bulk.

DuckDB provides a COPY FROM statement, which is used to ingest (bulk load) external data. External data can be delimited text, Parquet, or JSON files. You will learn the features of the COPY FROM statement.

Prerequisites

To learn the most from the book, you will need to be somewhat familiar with the idea of relational database and SQL (Structured Query Language). If you are not, you can get started with my other book, **Learning SQL in DuckDB: A Tutorial for Beginners.**

If you never use DuckDB's CLI, Appendix A will get you initiated. It also shows you how to install the CLI, which is all you need to create a DuckDB database and load data into database.

When you finish reading this book and trying its examples, you would have equipped yourself with the data ingestion skills ready to participate in real-world development projects.

Tutorials on Loading with COPY FROM statement

The most common delimited text file is CSV (Comma Separated Values). It is so named due to the use of a comma to separate (delimit) the fields of the text file.

We will load the following product.csv CSV file.

```
t001,tablet,2020-12-31,100.01
c002,cell,2020-10-01,200.22
d003,desktop,2020-08-15,300.00
l004,laptop,2020-01-10,400.40
p005,printer,2019-05-05,500.55
```

Records of the product.csv file will be loaded into the following DuckDB product table.

```
CREATE OR REPLACE TABLE product
 (p_code TEXT,
 p_name TEXT,
 p_date DATE,
 p_price DECIMAL);
```

To load product.csv to product table, we use a COPY statement as follows:

```
COPY product FROM 'product.csv';
```

The SELECT query in the following CLI screenshot shows the product.csv records were loaded correctly into the product table.

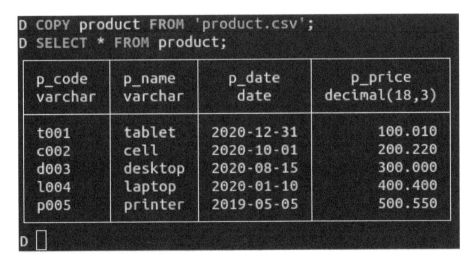

COPY is good only for existing table

COPY statement needs the target table to exist, otherwise it would fail.

Let's DROP the product table and try the COPY statement. We will get an error message saying that the product table does not exist.

```
D DROP TABLE product;
D copy product from 'abc.xyz';
Error: Catalog Error: Table with name product does not exist!
Did you mean "pg_proc"?
D
```

File extension can be anything

The file extension does need to be csv. The following example successfully load a csv file named with txt extension.

Here is the product.txt:

Note that the field delimiter is still comma; the difference between product.txt and product.csv is only only on their file extension.

The following CLI screenshot shows the COPY from product.txt and its result.

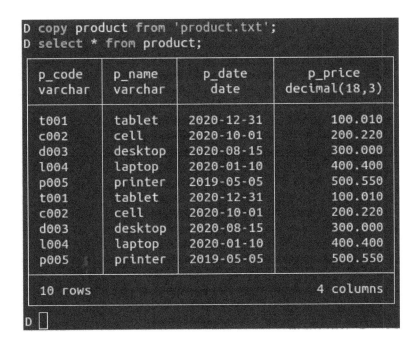

You might have noticed that I wrote SQL statements with different capitalization. They work well as **SQL statement is not case sensitive**.

File name can be anything

In fact you can have a different file name, not just the file extension.

Here is an example loading from abc.xyz file; the file is still comma delimited.

```
D copy product from 'abc.xyz';
D select * from product;
```

p_code varchar	p_name varchar	p_date date	p_price decimal(18,3)
t001	tablet	2020-12-31	100.010
c002	cell	2020-10-01	200.220
d003	desktop	2020-08-15	300.000
l004	laptop	2020-01-10	400.400
p005	printer	2019-05-05	500.550
t001	tablet	2020-12-31	100.010
c002	cell	2020-10-01	200.220
d003	desktop	2020-08-15	300.000
l004	laptop	2020-01-10	400.400
p005	printer	2019-05-05	500.550
t001	tablet	2020-12-31	100.010
c002	cell	2020-10-01	200.220
d003	desktop	2020-08-15	300.000
l004	laptop	2020-01-10	400.400
p005	printer	2019-05-05	500.550

15 rows	4 columns

D

COPY is adding (appending) rows

You might have noticed the COPY statements add rows; it does not have an option to update or replace existing rows.

The previous three COPY statements correctly resulted in 15 rows in the product table after loading, three times, the same 5 rows.

```
D select * from product;

 p_code     p_name     p_date         p_price
 varchar    varchar    date           decimal(18,3)

 t001       tablet     2020-12-31          100.010
 c002       cell       2020-10-01          200.220
 d003       desktop    2020-08-15          300.000
 l004       laptop     2020-01-10          400.400
 p005       printer    2019-05-05          500.550
 t001       tablet     2020-12-31          100.010
 c002       cell       2020-10-01          200.220
 d003       desktop    2020-08-15          300.000
 l004       laptop     2020-01-10          400.400
 p005       printer    2019-05-05          500.550
 t001       tablet     2020-12-31          100.010
 c002       cell       2020-10-01          200.220
 d003       desktop    2020-08-15          300.000
 l004       laptop     2020-01-10          400.400
 p005       printer    2019-05-05          500.550

 15 rows                                4 columns

D
```

Field Headers are not good

COPY will fail if you try to load the following product_header.csv

The field headers on the first row are incorrectly read as records; the date field in particular was the culprit.

```
D COPY product FROM 'product_header.csv';
Error: Invalid Input Error: date field value out of range: "date", expected form
at is (YYYY-MM-DD) at line 1 in column 2. Parser options:
  file=product_header.csv
  delimiter=',' (default)
  quote='"' (default)
  escape='"' (default)
  header=0' (default)
  sample_size=20480
  ignore_errors=0
  all_varchar=0
D
```

Delimiter does need to be a comma

What if the field delimiter of the file is not comma. Let's say we have the following product_pipe.txt has pipe delimiters.

Let's first empty the product table. (Printing a lot of rows waste space of this book pages)

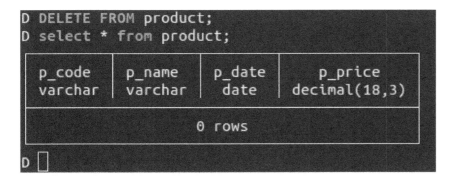

Trying to load the file will fail, as the COPY statement expects comma delimiter.

```
D COPY product FROM 'product_pipe.txt';
Error: Invalid Input Error: Error in file "product_pipe.txt" on line 2: expected
4 values per row, but got 1.
Parser options:
  file=product_pipe.txt
  delimiter=',' (default)
  quote='"' (default)
  escape='"' (default)
  header=0' (default)
  sample_size=20480
  ignore_errors=0
  all_varchar=0
D
```

To tell COPY that your delimiter is not comma, use DELIM option to indicate the delimiter.

The following CLI screenshot shows that the product_pipe.txt records have been successfully loaded into the product table.

```
D COPY product FROM 'product_pipe.txt' (DELIM '|');
D select * from product;

 p_code    p_name      p_date       p_price
 varchar   varchar      date       decimal(18,3)

 'pt001'   'tablet'    2020-12-31        100.010
 'pc002'   'cell'      2020-10-01        200.220
 'pd003'   'desktop'   2020-08-15        300.000
 'pl004'   'laptop'    2020-01-10        400.400
 'pp005'   'printer'   2019-05-05        500.550

D
```

Just a reminder, for comma delimiter you don't need to specify DELIM option, as comma is the DELIM default.

Loading Specific Columns

You might want to load the DuckDB table on some specific columns only.

Let's say we have the following csv file.

You can load the two fields into product table by specifying the two target columns: product(p_code, p_name), in the COPY statement.

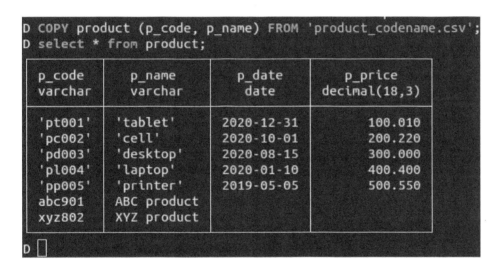

File Compression

If your file is big, you might have it compressed.

You can specify the compression type of the external file to import into the DuckDB table. Options are `none, gzip, zstd`.

Let's gzip compress our product.txt as follows:

```
djoni>gzip product.txt
djoni>
```

Now, use COPY FROM with compression sets to 'gzip' to import the product records. In the following example we empty the product table before importing.

```
D delete from product;
D copy product  from 'product.txt.gz' (format 'csv', compression 'gzip');
D select * from product;
```

p_code varchar	p_name varchar	p_date date	p_price decimal(6,2)
't001'	'tablet'	2020-12-31	100.01
'c002'	'cell'	2020-10-01	200.22
'd003'	'desktop'	2020-08-15	300.00
'l004'	'laptop'	2020-01-10	400.40
'p005'	'printer'	2019-05-05	500.55

```
D
```

JSON file

Below is an example of loading data from product.json.

```
Open          product.json          Save          □   ⊗
1 {"p_code":"K010","p_name":"keyboard","p_date":"2022-01-31","p_price":30}
2 {"p_code":"M011","p_name":"mouse","p_date":"2022-01-31","p_price":50.59}
3 {"p_code":"P022","p_name":"pen","p_date":"2022-01-31","p_price":300}
                JSON ▼  Tab Width: 8 ▼      Ln 3, Col 68    ▼    INS
```

The following COPY statement recognized the .json extension and interpret the file has JSON data, and successfully loaded the data.

```
D delete from product;
D COPY product FROM 'product.json';
D select * from product;
```

p_code varchar	p_name varchar	p_date date	p_price decimal(18,3)
K010	keyboard	2022-01-31	30.000
M011	mouse	2022-01-31	50.590
P022	pen	2022-01-31	300.000

```
D
```

If the file extension is not .json the COPY would fail.

```
D COPY product FROM 'product.jn';
Error: Invalid Input Error: Error in file "product.jn" on line 1: quote should b
e followed by end of value, end of row or another quote. (  file=product.jn
  delimiter=',' (default)
  quote='"' (default)
  escape='"' (default)
  header=0' (default)
  sample_size=20480
  ignore_errors=0
  all_varchar=0)
```

To avoid the failure, you can specify FORMAT 'json' as follows:

```
D COPY product FROM 'product.jn' (FORMAT 'json');
D select * from product;
```

p_code varchar	p_name varchar	p_date date	p_price decimal(18,3)
K010	keyboard	2022-01-31	30.000
M011	mouse	2022-01-31	50.590
P022	pen	2022-01-31	300.000
K010	keyboard	2022-01-31	30.000
M011	mouse	2022-01-31	50.590
P022	pen	2022-01-31	300.000

Parquet file

You can also load a parquet data.

In the following example we import data in a parquet file named p.pq. You can create the file using the COPY TO which will export the selected rows from the product table.

```
D COPY product TO 'p.pq' (FORMAT 'parquet');
D
```

Now that we have a parquet file, we can demonstrate the COPY FROM to load the parquet file.

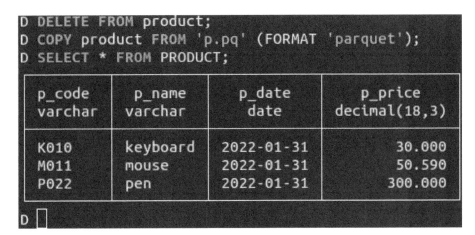

```
D DELETE FROM product;
D COPY product FROM 'p.pq' (FORMAT 'parquet');
D SELECT * FROM PRODUCT;
```

p_code varchar	p_name varchar	p_date date	p_price decimal(18,3)
K010	keyboard	2022-01-31	30.000
M011	mouse	2022-01-31	50.590
P022	pen	2022-01-31	300.000

```
D
```

Summary

You learned about COPY FROM statement and its various options to import text delimited files; as well, you have seen the application of the COPY FROM on JSON, and Parquet files.

You also learned COPY TO statement used to export to an external file, which can, similar to the COPY FROM, be text delimited, JSON, or Parquet. Appendix B has more about COPY TO.

Appendix A: Getting Started with CLI (Command Line Interface)

In this chapter you will download CLI and install it.

Downloading

Download CLI from https://duckdb.org/docs/installation/index
Select the installation zip file for your platform. In my case I selected the first one, Linux 64-bit.

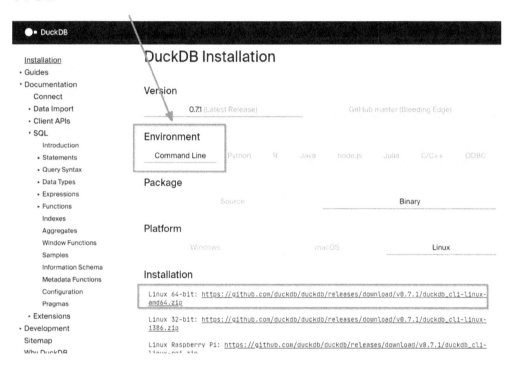

Installing

Extract the downloaded zip file into a folder of your choice. When extraction is completed, under that folder you should have a sub folder where you have a file **duckdb**.

That's all you need. You use this file to run CLI , and then create a database and all its object. **There's no database server to install and maintain.**

In my case, I extracted to CLI. So, in my Ubuntu terminal, I can see the duckdb like the following:

To start the duckdb CLI terminal, run the duckdb file as follows:

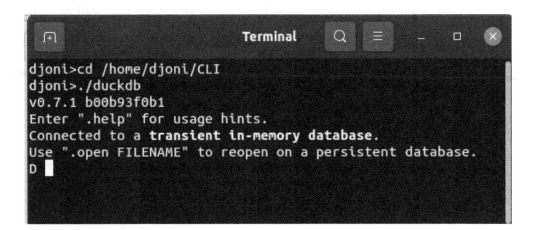

To create a new database, for example a database named book.duckdb, run the following. If the database already exists, it will be opened.

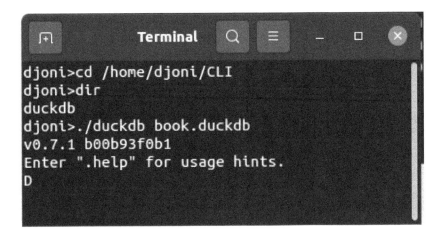

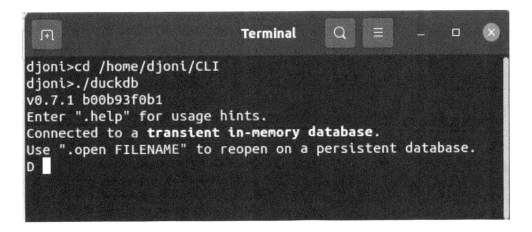

To exit DuckDB CLI, press ctrl + d. You will be back to your unix terminal.

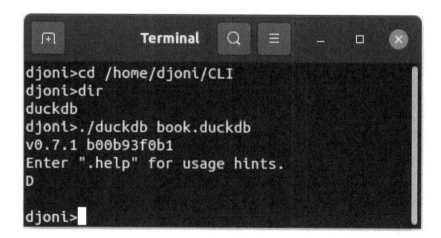

Now that you are on the DuckDB CLI, you can run SQL statement.

To start with, create a schema. Below I created a schema named **book_schema** in the **book** database. Don't forget to terminate your SQL with a semicolon.

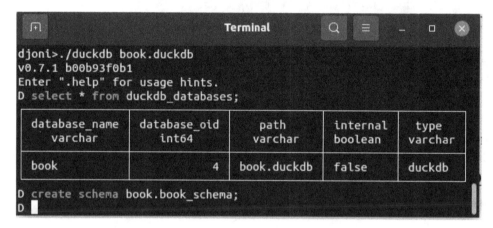

You can display the schema by running a select * from duckdb_schemas statement as follows:

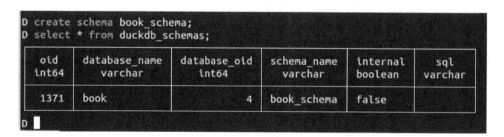

Next, let's create table named dummy with just one column, d of type integer. To confirm the table was created, you can query the duck_tables built in data dictionary's table duckdb_tables.

```
D create table dummy (d integer);
D select schema_name, table_name from duckdb_tables;
```

schema_name varchar	table_name varchar
main	dummy

The dummy table we just created is under the **main** schema. We actually wanted the table under our own schema, book_schema. We can do so by using a dot notation schemaname.tablename as follows.

```
D create table book_schema.dummy (d integer);
D select schema_name, table_name from duckdb_tables;
```

schema_name varchar	table_name varchar
book_schema	dummy
main	dummy

```
D
```

If you will often work with the book_schema, rather than prefixing with the schema-name, you can set book_schema as a **default** schema. Then when you create a table that you want it under the default schema, you don't need to specify the schema.

Below we set book_schema as the default schema. Then, we create dummy2 table with out specifying any schema. The dummy2 is created under book_schema.

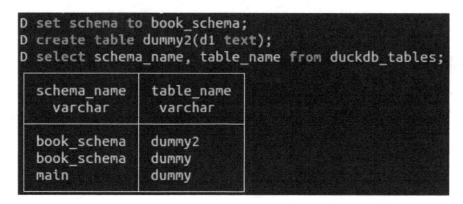

```
D set schema to book_schema;
D create table dummy2(d1 text);
D select schema_name, table_name from duckdb_tables;
```

schema_name varchar	table_name varchar
book_schema	dummy2
book_schema	dummy
main	dummy

This is the end of the Appendix and the book.

Good luck with applying your data ingestion skill.

Appendix B: COPY TO

The book is about data ingestion, bulk-loading external file into DuckDB table using COPY FROM.

This appendix talks about COPY TO lightly.

COPY TO is the opposite, it exports rows of a table to an external file, which can be text delimited, JSON, or Parquet.

Here is the syntax of the COPY TO statement:

```
COPY table-name TO file-name (format 'file-format')
```

Notice that the only difference from COPY FROM is the TO instead of FROM. Similar to that in COPY FROM, the file-format is CSV, JSON, or PARQUET.

Below is an example for CSV.

```
D copy product  to 'product_backup.txt' (format 'csv');
D 
```